Book of Poems

by DeArrius D. Rhymes

Book of Poems
By Dearrius Rhymes
Copyright 2021 by Dearrius Rhymes
Published By: Taylors Legacy LLC
All Rights Reserved

This book is a work of fiction. Names, characters, places, and incidents either are the product of the author's imagination or used fictitiously and are not to be constructed as real. Any resemblance to actual persons, living or dead, business establishments, events or locales, or, entirely coincidental. No Portion of this book may be used or reproduced in any manner whatsoever without written permission except in the case of brief quotations embodied in critical articles reviews.

TABLE OF CONTENTS

CHAPTER I	GOD		3
SOUL	With you		4
	Free eternity		5
	If…		6
	Makes Sense		7
	Tik Tok		8
CHAPTER II	Savory Love		11
BODY	Love Letter		12
	the little things		13
	Venom		14
	Follow my heart		15
	I miss You		16
	I Believe in You and Me		17
	Together		18
CHAPTER III	Suicide		20
MIND	Closed Book		21
	Silent Thoughts		22
	A long day		23
	Outta Town		24
	One thing at a time		25
	Half and Half		26
CHAPTER IV	*Freedom*		28
EMBRACE	Bless you		29
	Assassination		30
	Millionaires		31
	Target Practice		32
	Misjudged by god		33
CHAPTER V	Senior Will – 2017		35
TRUTH	A Man in 2020		36
	April Tenth, Two Thousand Twenty-One		37
	"Religion and Law"		38
	Once Fed – Juneteenth 2021		39
	Climax!		40

Chapter I

Soul

GOD

IS where my strength lies. Without Him,
I am a purposeless being in this world.

ALL by Himself. Infinite and immortal,
existing from everlasting to everlasting.

THE Creator of time. For Him, future is
past tense. What a mighty God we serve!

HELP in the time of trouble. He loves me,
even in times when I am not loving myself.

I long to see His face. "When we all get to
Heaven, what a day of rejoicing there will be."

NEED not to worry. Someday, I shall bow
before Him and forever behold His Glory!

With you

The same God yesterday,
today, and forevermore.

If tossed into a den of lions,
the Lord would let me lie there.
He would not hastily retrieve me,
because He will be there with me.

If tossed into a fiery furnace with
my brothers for his namesake,
He would not pull me out. But,
behold, He would not let me burn,
and He will be *there* with me!

I may face giants. But with God's armor
and a weapon tailored to my strengths,
I will win the war with the single draw of
a slingshot, merely because He is with me.

Through Life and death, He will be there.
I promise, if you believe God was, then
He is and He will always be with you.

Free eternity

Christians are still humans;
Christians are still sinners. But by
the blood of Jesus Christ and the grace
of the living God, we are made whole.

I was born into the same flesh as
those who believe not. However,
unlike them, I choose to accept
His offer of a Free eternity.

I am questioned about my faith;
I am forgiven through the
blood of Jesus Christ.

If…

If is a two-letter word that tends to intrigue a lot of hopeful imaginations. "If I had a million dollars then…"; "My day would be complete *if* I didn't have to work today"; "If this husband of mine did anything around the house…"

Google defines *if* as a word introducing a conditional clause…

"If my people, which are called by my name, shall humble themselves, and pray, and seek my face, and turn from their wicked ways; then will I hear from heaven, and will forgive their sin, and will heal their land."
2 Chronicles 7:14 KJV

Under the condition or supposing that we simply humble ourselves then pray to God, then turn from our wrong doings, the Lord declares He will not only hear and forgive us but heal our land - problems, grades, marriages, self!

Imagine: *If* we do our part, then our hopes and desires *will* become reality through God!

Makes Sense

The meadows and trees, the lakes and seas.
Four seasons filled with sunshine and rain.
Looks like Earth to me.

The winds whistle as the thunder booms.
Birds chirping and chickens crowing.
Sounds like Earth to me.

Rose bushes surrounding magnolia trees.
The stench of manure on the ground.
Smells Earth to me.

Sweet apples and tart cherries.
Grapes and wine, milk and honey.
Tastes Earth to me.

Laying on a beach daydreaming.
Laying in the grass sleeping.
Feels like Earth to me.

Life and death, blessings and curses.
Heaven residing with Hell; He created it.
That's Earth indeed!

Tik Tok

I am a timer, a clock;
with time winding down, ticking away.
When I was formed, my clock was full.
I've aged, the longer my clock has ticked;
the longer it ticks, the lower my timer gets.

There's only a matter of time,
before my time is up and then...
What might my clock say?
Will it never tick again?

I have seen others. They are timers
as well. Aren't we all just waiting?
Either waiting to run out of time,
or waiting until our time is fulfilled?

Who is He that begins the timer, and
how was I so fortunate to be *my* clock?
A clock full of life and time
and joy and peace and time
and hope and love and time.

Time and time again, I have seen
other as their timers have run out.
I have watched them in their last
hour, minute, second. And then,
there it is... Time is no more; their
time has simply run out. And now,
I have realized: until my timer has
no more time, until my clock fails

to tick again, I will use the time
I was given to my advantage.

I will give my time *back* to the One
who set my timer. I have realized,
the Timekeeper is why I have life
and time and joy and peace
and time and hope and love
and time. So, behold, I owe the
Timekeeper. And maybe, thereafter,
the Keeper of time will give me more
time – infinite perhaps – once my time
is fulfilled…

Chapter II

Body

Savory Love

Just as the sun is bound to set,
Even the sweetest rose won't live forever.
Yet, the sun will rise every day again and again,
And so shall our savory love.

Time and value, patience and grace;
Love has many qualities all in one.
May every day be filled with each of them,
As destined by hope, harmony, and peace.

The light may dim and the road may wither
Along the way, but the path shall remain.
For as the sun rises no matter the day,
So shall our perpetual love do the same.

Love Letter

Dear Love,

Leading me in this direction, but why?
Only to be filled and emptied once more?
Valuing me and then casting me aside again;
Entangling my emotions in a fairytale?

Learning to not make the same mistakes;
Obviously guarding my heart, now.
Vowing to never come across you again;
Even once more, I fall into your arms.

Living life remains priceless.
Obligating myself to you this time.
Very carefully, I will pursue you;
Expecting the best, always.

Love,
Me

the little things

"it's the little things that count! The
little things are why I love you!" All
of this, she exclaimed to me. And
somehow, they seem to matter more.

a date - dinner and a movie. My
pockets run flat, all to satisfy her. All
to show how much I truly love her. Yet,
she only remembers the slightest details.

at dinner: I failed to compliment her hair. At
the movie: I held her hand the wrong way. I
am now convinced about the little things. For
they are more significant towards my peace.

i've learned to listen to her miniscule desires. I
realized the worth and value of a penny. Trust
and believe, remember and do tell. For:
IT'S THE LITTLE THINGS THAT COUNT!

Venom

The wicked poison,
a fatal ending it induces.
How sweet it must be.

Like the nectar of a flower,
like milk and honey flowing
through The Promised Land.

While despised by others,
it means life or death
for the beholder.

Whether it be to feast,
to protect one's self or
to simply gain the upper hand.

One lethal injection and what
once was, becomes none. Venom,
She is, and I am the serpent.

Follow my heart

I was told to follow my heart… I realized my feelings for you were even greater when you insisted we take a step back because my heart actually dropped.

My heart began looking forward to your name coming across the screen of my phone. It was rejuvenated by the thought of getting closer to you. And following my heart would be embarking on a journey with someone who checks all the boxes. My flesh wants me to remain in the situation I'm in because of all the time, money, and *stuff* that has been put into it.

What I do know no matter what, though, is that: God is very intentional; anything I have with you, I want it to be special and done right; and I know what real love looks like. I see the future we could have, but for now, I agree, the best decision is for us to take a step back. I agree that I don't want to force anything. And real *Love* is understanding that if we're meant to be, we will be when the time is right.

I miss You

I'm here, away from
You, and now I know that
I miss You most – more
than I've ever missed You
or anyone else before!

Wow… I realize, now,
that I love You more than
anyone I've ever loved.
You, as You are; You,
no matter the circumstance.

I miss You dearly, more
than I ever thought I would.
And someday, I'll change
your last name, unless
I've missed the chance?

I Believe in You and Me

I'm not sure where life will take you or me, but it is my hope and desire to take every next step we make together.

My greatest untold secret is that I love fairytales; and although I once told you once that those were fictional, I finally believe in you and me. Now, I long to write a nonfiction fairytale with you. I want you to adore me as the man of your dreams again, your knight in shining armor who swept you off your feet into a happily ever after!

The songs you loved to listen to that made you feel every great thing you once imagined about us, I want you to mesmerize over the thought of them again. This time, however, I want to do everything in the right and best way possible.

Am I perfect? No, and as sure as we continue to live and grow together, we will have our days. And although I may not be perfect, if you asked me, "Am I complete?" right now, my answer would still be "No"… That is only unless you say, "Yes" to being my other half?

*Inspired by my **Love for Her***
June 3, 2021

Together

I love that about us! Through thin, thick & thicker we've been there for each other. Even at times when it seemed like our love no longer remained, we remained, together.

I will admit that about us! We have our days. Yet, honestly, we'd still have our days even if we were apart. So, we work it out and strive and pray for better days. This is because we believe, if love is meant to be, so shall we always be, together.

I cherish that about us! The bond we have is imperishable. Man will doubt and envy our intramolecular covalent connection. Heaven has prepared us mansions, side by side. Even there we shall inseparably reside in a paired abode, together.

Chapter III

Mind

Suicide

Don't do it! There is definitely another way. You can
Overcome your life's perplexing circumstances.
Never choose to make a permanent decision in a
Temporary situation. Please don't. Hear me out!

Get up! You have too much on the line to simply throw
In the towel now. You have a life worth living, a life with
Value that should not be exchanged for a reluctant death.
Even though it's easy to quit, See It Through, please!

Understand that "You are loved!" Believe me. Just keep
Pressing forward until you have completely run life's course!

Closed Book

Open up to me.
Your words are sincere,
but I have no chance
of truly knowing them.

Your thoughts are hidden.
Every day, you swallow
the mental key to the divine
treasures that lie within your mind.

Open up to me, please!
Do not overflow your
mental capacity with weary
waves of worry and untold truths.

I await at the edge of your pages.
I long to manifest the fine print of
your submerged intelligence. Share,
with me, your knowledge and wisdom.

Silent Thoughts

I sit here and think, silently.

They talk, laugh, and joke around.
I watch, observe, and occasionally smile.

In my own silence, I mediate
and annotate. *We* analyze ignorance
from a mile away – I talk to the voice
that listens to my abstract gossip.

Vivid images appear; I envision indescribable
scenarios. Some are to be shared – though they
won't be, unless it's with me, silently. A great
deal would call it selfish, but the wise know.
They too have their own thoughts – copious
opinions, beliefs, and ideas I'll never know.
But it's all fair game, because the atmosphere
awaits and preys on the tongue's utterance.

A long day

24 hours.
1440 minutes.
86,400 seconds.
What a long day...

A meeting and a migraine.
Only time to gobble breakfast,
then dinner and take a shower,
not even simmer. What a long day...

Reflections become dreams,
as my jeans become pajamas.
Enough time for everything, yet
no time to breathe. What a long day…

Outta Town

Go away, venture out.
It's time to get outta town!

Too much going on, I know.
Those who may understand
are sometimes away in places
far from your humble abode.

I'm tellin' you; it's bout that time.
Go on, and get outta town!

Liberate yourself from the past
that hunts you like a Mississippi
redneck. You can always come
back, but you'll be much better.

And once you've *got* gone, stay gone,
merely long enough to come back!

Gettin' gone grants an exhilarating
voyage that prepares a royal return in
honor of your awaited arrival, as you
ride into town on the back of a donkey.

So, go on, and get outta town. And when
you get back, you'll sore like an eagle!

One thing at a time

Slow down. Crawl while you can,
because, soon, you'll naturally walk.
Learn to run after having walked
a mile. Take it one day at a time.

It's all in your head. Someone told
you to catch up, and now you're
rushing instead. Run the race at your
own pace. Set the tone and finish strong.

I told you once and I'll tell you again:
Slow down; it's all in your head.
Just finish strong in the end. Learn to
take things: One thing at a time.

Take advantage while you can, and,
trust, you'll never run out of time!

Half and Half

What a dream it is to be complete. Oh,
to be whole and at your fullest capacity.

A half-empty glass is the result of a needed
sip or an empty void waiting to be filled.

A half-full glass is the illusion formed by
the wise for those who seek content joy.

In every situation, there is good and bad,
but the magnitude of hurt or happiness will
depend on the nature of one's limbic system.

For there is no such thing as a half-empty or
half-full glass; the two reside in harmonic peace,
balancing the wonderful and weary waves
of life as we *understand* it.

So be it, a man cannot survive in a desert
without water, and he will surely breath a
final breathe if consumed in a body of it.

In the end, to be whole is to have half and half.
For a *perfect* being, with the exemption of Christ,
is merely one who has learned from merely half
of life's mishaps along the way.

Chapter IV

Embrace

Freedom

Emancipation -
Peace n justice?
Harriet Tubman
Show us the way

    Jim Crow –
    New sheriff in town.
    Lie of the land,
    Nails in our hands!

        Black n brown –
        A crown of thorns,
        A heavy cross to bear.
        Salvation where you at?

Bless you

"Achoo," I sneezed;
The trigger, they squeezed.
The police just shot me.
Call 9-1-1 please!

Some kill for sport,
Then win in court.
Our blessings, cut short,
So they remain invincible.

Amazing grace,
Save a race.
Cut the trial,
And end the case.

I walk and I pace,
Looking at my Black son's face.
I watch them place
Me six feet under.

Lord, help us please;
We're all on our knees!
All they had to do was say,
"Bless you" when I sneezed.

Assassination

Throughout midair, I travel
faster than lightning,
at the speed of God himself.
Is it fair to the soul of whom I approach?

I am almost there. I can hear
the progressiveness in the voice
of my victim. A sudden death.
Am I the one to blame?

I was merely released from the
chamber. I can see their sweat, but
I am not ready to do this.
Who pulled the trigger?

What hatred one must have to
put *me* in the middle of their
envious ways. They did nothing wrong.
Why must tragedy be the result?

A *bang* and a *clap* all in one! From
one second to the next, another
life claimed, again. As blood sheds,
I am content; for I am only the tool.

Millionaires

It's hard tah let go
of em ain't it?

Them machines out there
pickin ya cotton, makin
ya a millionaire.

If I was you, I guess I wouldn't
let go of em either.

But maybe I'd a'least treat em
wit a lil respect. Maybe I'd
even let em read n write.

Then again, I guess if ya did that,
you wouldn't be a millionaire huh?

I guess ya did right. Imagine the
man out there plantin and pickin also
havin the knowledge to sell his own.

Power and promise, but not in your land.
Hmm, Millionaires, *they* were indeed.

Target Practice

Brothers killing brothers.
"Twelve" killing brothers.

Fathers beating mothers.
System beating fathers.

Family stopped praying.
Devil starts preying.

Single mother needs a loan.
Lights out, food gone.

Kid grows, sells drugs.
A school boy, now a thug.

Bullseye on their backs.
Black skin on their backs.

It's not fair – the life we live.
"Life's not fair" – advice they give.

Let's keep it real.
Something's gotta chill.

Why are we the target?
Practice ends here!

Misjudged by god

My ancestors worshipped you because
they had to, for they realized they had no
   choice. They smiled while verbally glorifying
      you and mentally damning you, for my
         namesake.

The Civil War resulted in their favor,
yet their freedom resulted in segregation –
legal treason. A taste of god's water got
   them smote, and one word of good trouble
         got them smoked.

You walk by me eyes-front, straight-faced,
purse-clinched at a steady pace. And later,
you laugh because you know I'm still
fighting for freedom. Yea though I walk
  through the valley of the shadow of America,
  I will not fear you in the twenty-first century.

Suited and booted, Trump and Chauvin.
We're winning, they're losing. Let's keep
   it that way, in order to form a more perfect
   nation with liberty and justice for all of us
      who deserve the two.

Chapter V

Truth

Senior Will – 2017

The *past* is done;
however, now is promised...
So, let's promise ourselves
a greater future now,
however we can,
by learning from
whatever we've done
and moving *passed* it."

A Man in 2020

A man says, "It feels like we're living in the textbooks right now...

Everything we write, draw, speak and *start* will be written in the textbooks of what the masses did before, during and after all of this is over."

We are living in a moment of history, a renaissance, a time in which the entire world will look back in awe of us and everything we accomplished.

"... Cease your moment and create and produce like never before!"

Inspired by ***Tyler O. Yarbrough***

April Tenth, Two Thousand Twenty-One

Had four or five lab reports due.
I was worried about submitting
applications to graduate programs.
On the bright side, I met the
infamous James Meredith for the
First time – how amazing he was!

Knew more at eighty-seven years old
than I ever believed a man could truly
know. During dinner, I wondered, *Is this
really him, or is this all one big (sweet) dream?*
Lucky for me this was reality. It was him,
and what a man he was!

Think the thing I will always remember
is his serious sense of humor. He told
me,"Ain't no fool like an old fool, and I'll let
you make what you want of that." Most
importantly he told me, "God don't make no
mistakes!" Thank you, James, for your
wisdom.

"Religion and Law"

A wise man was fortunate to
know a seasoned wise man.

"In God We Trust," said
America. A country built
on the basis of Religion.

America made up a great
deal of inhumane regulations
to *legally* suppress a Race of
chosen people by Law.

Religion and Law coincide
in a way that can only be
elucidated by the *most important*
speech to ever be written –
"Religion and Law" by James Meredith.

Once Fed – Juneteenth 2021

Joe Biden, the Vice President who stood alongside Barack
and now the President who granted Kamala
her grand opportunity to be placed in the
same history book.

Thank you for recognizing the freedoms of slavery as a
national holiday. No, thank you to America; if it chooses
to stop with the federal symbolization of honoring
its reluctant release of my ancestors.

I am a Black man in America and I am still hungry.
The need to fight for equality or equity is an insult
to the pride of my moral and natural existence.
The battle is not over and it never will be;
feed us more.

If we were only fed a few times in our life, we
would've been dead before knowing our names.
Juneteenth is my morning bowl of cereal for
one of 365 days.

They say defund the police; I say incarcerate the judges
and prosecutors that pat murderous cops on the
wrist and conclude the lives of black men
for the use of natural herbs.

Climax!

Once one takes care of the Soul, that individual can begin to tranquilly handle the cares of this chaotic world with contentment. Succeeding that, one must then understand the importance of the Body and take care of its most relevant organ. For without the heart, eternity would have no flow.

Moreover, one should strive to positively and unconditionally preserve the Mind. For without it, the previous articles mean nothing because there is no thoughtfulness towards the processes required for life's progression.

As one accepts the challenge to Embrace society's broken system in honesty and unveil the Truth, one can subsequently engage in the forwardness of the entire world, though peace on Earth will never be achieved because there will always be a (necessary) time for war(s).

Ultimately, upon choosing to take care of one's self and meticulously evaluating the relevance of history's past, present, and near future, *you* can then participate in the aiding of others to also reach an immortal-like Climax!

Made in the USA
Columbia, SC
27 June 2023

19487594R00024